HANDWRITING Pocketbook

By Julie Bennett

Cartoons:
Phil Hailstone

Published by:

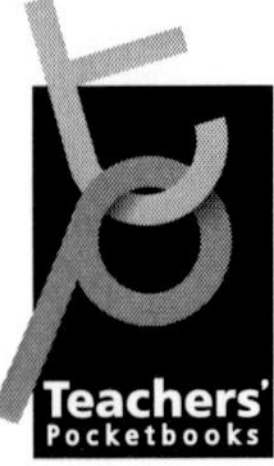

Teachers' Pocketbooks
Laurel House, Station Approach,
Alresford, Hampshire SO24 9JH, UK
Tel: +44 (0)1962 735573
Fax: +44 (0)1962 733637
E-mail: sales@teacherspocketbooks.co.uk
Website: www.teacherspocketbooks.co.uk

Teachers' Pocketbooks is an imprint of Management Pocketbooks Ltd.

Series editor – Linda Edge.

This edition published 2007. Reprinted 2013

ISBN 978 1 903776 76 6

British Library Cataloguing-in-Publication Data – A catalogue record for this book is available from the British Library.

Design, typesetting and graphics by Efex Ltd.
Printed in UK.

Contents

Introduction

Why a book on handwriting? In this technological age, don't computers eliminate the necessity for handwritten script? Technology has made an enormous contribution to the world of education – and the benefits of word-processing are unquestionable. But handwriting still offers some things that computers cannot, and as two primary school pupils point out:

'We mustn't always rely on machines.' (9 yrs)
'We need to keep doing handwriting in case we forget how to do it.' (7 yrs)

Students use handwriting for between 30% and 60% of classroom time; it is still the main method of jotting down notes, capturing ideas and of recording evidence of learning in school and in external examinations.

Introduction

Handwriting has played an important part in human history and communication. Scribes have been held in high esteem across cultures and across centuries for their ability to weave **beauty** into our written language. It's easy to see that there's an **aesthetic** aspect to handwriting for both reader and writer.

There is also something very **personal** about handwriting. A handwritten letter offers a personal touch and represents an **investment of self**.

Being personally involved in the **fluent**, **creative process** of handwriting gives us a sense of **ownership**, **pride** and **resourcefulness**.

Perhaps more than that, handwriting is an expression of **identity**. As a teenager, I remember experimenting with elements of other people's writing and making them my own. I took the roundness of my mother's hand, the uniformity of my father's, the slant and neatness of my friend Vince's script, Mr Eagles' funny 'ℰ's', and later I took inspiration from the italicised style of Steve Varley, my university lecturer. Our handwriting style **evolves**. It grows up with us and it's **unique** to us.

Introduction

When I first started teaching 20 years ago, I found that, despite a structured approach, achieving acceptable handwriting was a stumbling block for many learners.

When I later began working with students who had specific learning difficulties, I found many of them struggled with handwriting. This caused them so many additional problems that it led me on a quest to discover the specific reasons for handwriting difficulties, and how they might be overcome.

This book is the result of that quest. It is designed to offer ideas and resources on handwriting for **teachers**, **teaching assistants** and **parents**. It covers issues that arise in both the formal teaching of handwriting and in the informal opportunities for improving handwriting that occur during the school day or at home. You'll find it useful whether you're teaching beginner writers or improving and troubleshooting handwriting problems with older students.

Adopting some of the ideas here will enable you to understand and support your students as they learn and improve their handwriting.

Handwriting Matters

The problems

In our classrooms we have the responsibility for teaching and/or improving students' handwriting. We regularly encounter students whose handwriting is:

- Slow
- Illegible
- Poorly formed
- Joined incorrectly
- Lacking in fluency
- A mixture of capitals and lower case
- A mixture of cursive (joined) and print (not joined)
- Sloping in multiple directions
- Not uniform in size/too large/too small

These difficulties may be a result of developmental delay or specific learning difficulty, or they may simply be habitual patterns that have developed over time. Whatever the causes, learners with handwriting difficulties often have to invest an enormous amount of effort to create acceptable handwriting. As a result they may experience tiredness, frustration and may possibly get 'turned off' from learning.

 **Struggling with handwriting hinders learning and achievement.** 

What are the benefits?

It is beneficial to work towards improving handwriting for both our students and ourselves.

Some benefits of fluent and legible handwriting are:

- Ease of learning letter strings and spellings
- Higher exam results
- Better readability for teachers and examiners (time saving for teachers)
- Easier acceptance of students' ideas because they are more easily read
- Enhanced ability to focus on composition and quality of writing content
- Improved capacity of writers to access their own thoughts and information
- Raised sense of self-competence as writers, which in turn increases achievement across all subjects

It is important that we work towards improving our students' level of handwriting, as it will improve their overall performance.

What is handwriting?

Handwriting is not an isolated activity; neither can it be seen solely as a motor activity (all about movement). It is part of language activity. Virginia Berninger refers to handwriting as 'language by hand', which is a useful reminder of its context and purpose.

Reading =  Language by eye

Listening =  Language by ear

Speaking =  Language by mouth

Writing =  Language by hand

Handwriting should be seen in the context of its place in literacy development. We know that the most effective methods for teaching literacy are structured, cumulative, and multi-sensory; it is the same for handwriting. First we must be clear about what we are teaching and expecting from our writers.

Defining 'good handwriting'

As teachers we often refer to 'good handwriting'. It is important to define what the qualities of good handwriting are before we start to teach it. There are three broad goals:

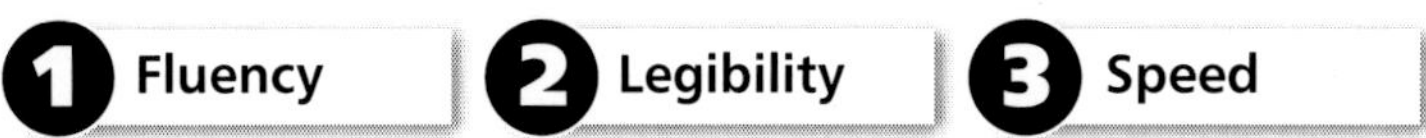

Fluency is the ability to carry out the motor movements required for handwriting smoothly, easily, comfortably and readily.

Legibility is the ease with which the reader (and the writer) can discern the handwriting on the page and is directly related to how well formed the letters are.

Speed is the rate at which handwriting is produced in relation to a student's developmental stage.

The body, mind and soul of handwriting

To achieve fluency, legibility and speed we need to engage the:

The Body: Getting the position and the motor movements of handwriting physically correct.

The Mind: Understanding the construction of handwriting and the meaning of the language we are writing.

The Soul: Enjoying the process, developing a sensual and aesthetic appreciation of handwriting.

Used with kind permission of Melvyn Ramsden www.realspelling.com

Body, mind and soul

'Good handwriting is so
important for getting your
ideas across.
For me, writing includes
the **heart** and the **head** as well
as the **hand**.'

Roger McGough, Poet

The internal model of handwriting

There are two key processes – related but different – that come into action for handwriting. Try this brief activity to help you experience them both:

Activity:

Sign your name on a piece of paper, first with your eyes open and then again with your eyes closed. What do you notice?

1. The first time you relied on **visual feedback**.
2. The second time you relied on **kinaesthetic feedback** (the feel and movement).

The key to fluency lies with **kinaesthetic feedback**. Visual feedback is not rhythmic; kinaesthetic feedback is. By using kinaesthetic feedback we develop an **internal representation** of handwriting. One effective method of teaching and improving handwriting is to teach the **rhythmic**, **fluent**, **(kinaesthetic) movement** sequences which build the internal model.

Handwriting: the ultimate goal

Legible and fluent handwriting is achieved by creating and building on an effective internal model. It's a process of condensing and transforming the complex, discrete movements of handwriting into an automatic process called 'grapho-motor control'.

Ultimately we are aiming for what A. R. Luria (a Soviet neuropsychologist) called:

'Kinetic Melody'

Kinetic Melody is the ability to perform all the complex tasks which make up the skill of handwriting in one automatic, fluent motion.

Handwriting: the ultimate goal

The complex task of handwriting includes a wide range of cognitive, perceptual, motor and linguistic skills. 'Good handwriting' is a product of all these aspects automatically working together in harmony.

This book will show you how to:

- Nurture the '**kinetic melody**'
- Take into account 'the **body**, **mind** and **soul**'
- Achieve **fluency**, **legibility** and, consequently, appropriate **speed** for handwriting

Before looking at the best way to teach good handwriting we should consider the role of a school handwriting policy. It is this that sets the context for both learners and teachers.

Handwriting Policy

Developing a school handwriting policy

A well thought-out policy will give your school **guidelines** from which to effectively teach handwriting. A handwriting policy is relevant for early years, primary and secondary settings. It sets the **context** and **culture** and promotes **consistency** throughout the school.

It should, among other things, encourage a positive partnership between home and school, and promote consistent marking feedback.

The development and detail of a handwriting policy is largely down to the individual school. It will take into account national guidelines and meet the needs of a school's particular intake. There is not space to do it justice here, but three of the key aspects to consider are covered in the next few pages:

1. Scheme.
2. Script.
3. Consistency of language.

If you are developing a handwriting policy, you may find The National Handwriting Association's book *Developing a Handwriting Policy for your School* useful.

Which scheme?

Many – though not all – schools choose to adopt a **handwriting scheme**. By 'scheme' I mean a set of resources which includes materials for the structured teaching of handwriting skills. Schemes usually progress from teaching single letter forms to fluent, cursive script.

An excellent reference for help with choosing a school handwriting scheme is The National Handwriting Association's publication:

Which Handwriting Scheme?: A review of currently available publications
Ed. Gwen Dornan and Jane Taylor

It reviews current schemes, giving an outline of content with comments from experts in the handwriting field. Whichever scheme you decide on, ensure that it is consistent, structured and cumulative.

Which script?

The style of script you use to teach handwriting, and how this fits within your school scheme or policy, will determine how you use the handwriting criteria outlined later in this chapter.

In some counties and regions the local authority chooses the handwriting style; in others, schools are free to choose both style and scheme. Whichever method is used, provision for those with specific learning difficulties or specific motor control difficulties should be made.

It's worth noting that some letter formations and joins differ from script to script. When different styles are taught within the same school it can lead to confusion for pupils. So consistency and continuity within a school are important.

It goes beyond the remit of this book to consider choice of script in depth here, but the following pages present some of the key factors in making your decision.

Cursive: the benefits

'Cursive' is another term for 'joined up' writing. Research has shown that using cursive script has a positive impact on handwriting and a helpful widespread educational impact.

Cursive Writing
improves
flow
motor rhythm
speed
fluency
efficiency
style
maturity
reinforces
multisensory learning
spelling patterns
encourages
wholewords
focus
see
feel
aids
movement
left to right
reduces
reversals
inversions
stress
decreasing memory task

Print to cursive

There are differing opinions as to whether writing should be taught from the outset as: **print**, **print with entry and exit strokes**, or as **cursive**.

Although there are various criticisms of it for classroom use, I have included an example of italic writing. Italic writing requires specialist teaching and the precision required for its exact form means it may not serve students well as an efficient, everyday handwriting style. There is, however, an argument for it being a good foundation to work from, and its beauty can not be denied.

Script type	What it looks like
Print/Stick and ball/ Manuscript style	The quick brown fox jumps over a lazy dog.
Entry and exit strokes/Pre- cursive/ Print with ligatures	The quick brown fox jumps over a lazy dog.
Italic	The quick brown fox jumps over a lazy dog.
Cursive/Joined up	The quick brown fox jumps over a lazy dog.

Cursive from the start?

It makes sense to aim for an efficient, mature, cursive handwriting style in adulthood, but should children be taught 'joined-up writing' right from the start?

Some of the concerns about teaching cursive from the outset are:

- The **entry and exit strokes** may be seen by beginner writers to be an **integral part** of the letters, causing confusion and leading to further writing problems
- Beginner writers may not be **developmentally** ready for cursive writing

The benefits of cursive writing (increased speed, flow, style, etc) suggest it is valuable to teach it as soon as possible once the correct movement of the letter formations is known.

Describing handwriting

Once the scheme and style of handwriting have been chosen, a key point is to ensure that everyone uses the same terminology to describe different elements of the written language. The diagram below illustrates some of the appropriate terms:

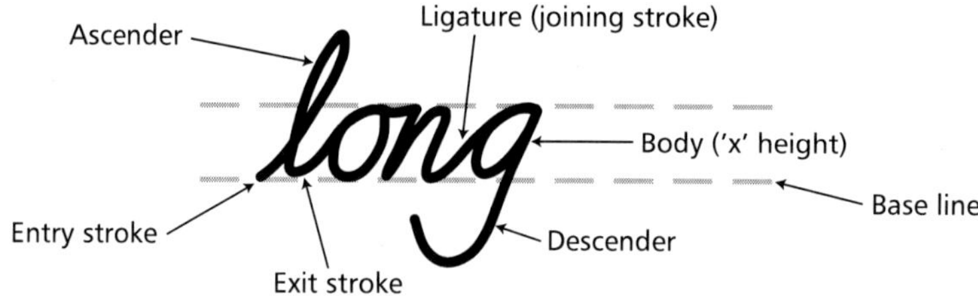

Having established a policy, your school will have the framework within which to offer a consistent and structured approach to handwriting.

Are You Sitting Comfortably?

Setting up

The previous chapters looked at theory and policy. Pages 41-58 will fix the handwriting goalposts to supply a thorough checklist for teaching, improving and troubleshooting handwriting, but first: **Are you sitting comfortably?**

Setting up correctly for handwriting is a crucial first step towards fluency. It relates to physical comfort (remember **body**, mind and soul?) and includes:

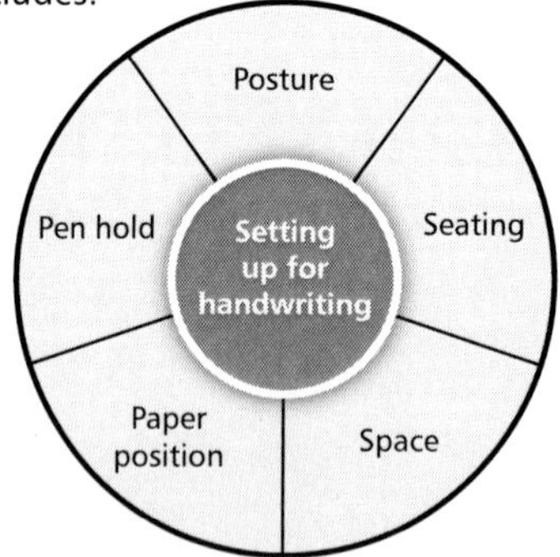

In the average classroom there will be both left- and right-handed children. The 'handedness' of a child will have an impact on posture, seating, space, paper position, pen hold, handwriting instruction. (This book offers ways of assisting both left- and right-handed learners to improve their handwriting but for specific issues facing left-handed writers see pages 101-102 and for left-handed resources see pages 114-115.)

Body in balance

The secret to sitting comfortably while writing is to attain a neutral, stable posture; one that distributes weight evenly and brings harmony and balance to the body. Sometimes, when writing, students complain of particular aches and pains that are a result of irregularities in their posture. More often than not these writers have simply developed **unhelpful posture habits** but sometimes their discomfort can be indicative of underlying medical problems.

If you are concerned about the possibility that there may be an underlying medical cause for a child's discomfort, refer to an appropriate professional, eg SENCO, educational psychologist, child development centre or the child's GP.

Ideal seating position

Ideally, when teaching handwriting:

- The writer should be positioned square to the table, feet flat on the ground, knees at a 90 degree angle and elbows at the height of the desk top
- The writing surface should be stable
- If the desk is too low, raise its height; if it's too high, use a footrest and raise the seat height

Co-ordinated movements

Handwriting involves a complex combination of co-ordinated movements. Some children have particular difficulty with the physical movements. This may be because of physical control, perceptual difficulties, or a combination of both. Anne Markee, a senior community physiotherapist, has produced a leaflet, *Hands Up for Handwriting* which includes a series of exercises to help develop the physical skills for writing. It is available from the National Handwriting Association. There are seven groups from which to select exercises:

- Shoulders
- Elbows
- Wrists and fists
- Flat hands
- Fingers and thumbs
- Pencil power
- Grasp and grip

Students who are dyspraxic are likely to have difficulty with motor co-ordination for handwriting. (See page 97 for more information.)

Space: left and right

Both left- and right-handed students need a suitable space to work in with sufficient room for the **paper** and the **movement of their writing arm**. Consideration needs to be given to which side of a desk students sit to avoid problems of cramped workspace:

1. Right-handed students – most of the movement will be to the **right** of the midline of their body. They need **space to their right**.

2. Left-handed students – most of the movement will be to the **left** of the midline of their body. They need **space to their left**.

- The best position for a **left-handed student** is **to the right of their individual writing space** this creates a good amount of working space to their **left**
- If they are sharing a desk or are in a row of tables, left-handers need to be seated on the left of the desk or else seated next to another left hander
- Do not seat a left-hander to the right of a right-hander. It results in 'elbow clash' or restricted movement

Paper position

The position of the paper affects the writer's posture:

Left-handed writer

The page should be rotated slightly clockwise when writing.

Right-handed writer

The page should be rotated slightly anti-clockwise when writing.

Note that the non-writing hand is in a supportive position to maintain the paper position.

Is there a 'correct' pen/pencil hold?

How students hold their pen or pencil can significantly affect their writing. Once established, even the most uncomfortable pen hold is difficult to alter. Writers should be taught to use a pen hold which fosters efficient, comfortable handwriting, one that supports comfortable body balance and promotes kinetic melody.

For many years accepted wisdom in schools has been that a conventional pen hold, the 'dynamic tripod' grip (see page 34), should be taught to all students. It has been commonly thought that not using this hold can affect: fluency, neatness, speed and legibility. However, recent research challenges the notion of a 'correct' pen hold. Some of the research shows no differences in legibility, fatigue, strength or speed of writing when children use non-traditional pen holds.

Another finding is that changes in pen hold occur with maturity. Notably, children develop the maturity to hold a pen with the dynamic tripod grip between the ages of 4-6 years.

Is there only one ‘good’ pen/pencil hold?

When it is developmentally appropriate, you can teach children to use the dynamic tripod grip. Generally, this offers writers a good body balance, control for accuracy, and fluency of movement. However, do view the notion of ‘correct’ pen hold with some flexibility.

There is a wide range of pens and pencils on the market now with various barrel sizes, rubber grips, nibs and shapes, all of which can affect pen hold. Keep in mind the goals of **fluency**, **legibility**, and **appropriate speed** when choosing pens and when teaching and adjusting pen holds.

The following pages show the dynamic tripod and an effective alternative grip.

The dynamic tripod grip

The dynamic tripod is the conventional pen hold, using index finger, middle finger and thumb. The index finger sits on top of the pen barrel. The pen is held between the pads of the thumb and index finger, with the middle finger underneath.

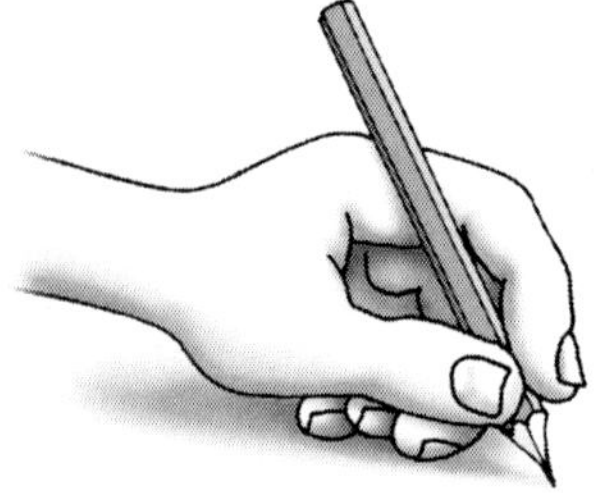

Dynamic tripod – left hand

Dynamic tripod – right hand

The pen/pencil should be held at about 2 cm from the point.

An alternative grip

Rosemary Sassoon has researched effective, ineffective and alternative pen holds. You can find out more about pen hold variations from her book *Handwriting Problems in the Secondary School* (see page 125). It is possible to create fluent, legible handwriting, of appropriate speed, with an effective, alternative pen hold. What makes for 'effective' is good **control** and good level of **comfort**. Below is an example of an effective alternative pen grip.

Choosing a pen or pencil

When choosing writing tools take into account the following:

- Quality and thickness of the lead, ink or nib (this can dramatically affect the quality of writing)
- Thickness of the barrel (this can affect pen hold)
- Length (avoid really stubby short pens/pencils. Half-length pencils can be beneficial for some children. Generally the writing implement should be long enough to reach over the web of the thumb)
- Overall comfort and how the tool lends itself to being held/gripped by the writer

Traditionally beginner writers start with pencils; however there is no evidence to suggest a particular benefit in using chunky 'infant' pencils.

Pencil toppers

Discourage students from using pencil toppers. They look good and children are attracted by them, but they weigh the pen/pencil down and change the angle of hold.

Get a grip

People have their own preferred style of pen or pencil. Some are especially designed to assist with correcting or maintaining the dynamic tripod grip. You might be interested to investigate:

- **The Yoropen** (pen and pencil: suitable for left- and right-handers)
- **Stabilo 's move easy** (pen and pencil: left-handed and right-handed versions)
- **Easyriter** (pen and pencil: suitable for left- and right-handers)

For further information on these and other pens and pencils see page 113.

You can also buy commercially produced rubber or plastic grips designed to fit over an ordinary pen or pencil. (See page 112.)

The selection of both writing tools and grips should be dependent on a combination of comfort of the writer, effective pen hold, fluency and control.

Getting the tension right

Sometimes writers tense their fingers, hands and arms when writing. Too much tension can cause pain in the thumb, fingers, hand and arm. You can assist students to recognise tension in writing.

Is the pen hold too tight? Ask your students to hold tightly a (real or imagined) small stone in their fingertips. Move on to holding gently a (real or imagined) feather in their fingertips. Each time, discuss how their hands and arms feel. This activity offers an opportunity for you to illustrate to your students how they can write more quickly and for a longer time when their hands are relaxed.

Is the hand held in too tight a fist? Ask your students to hold an imaginary round ball inside their hand as they write, or scrunch up a piece of A4 paper into a small ball and ask them to hold this inside their writing hand as they write.

Used with kind permission of Kim Stitzer from www.drawyourworld.com

Getting it all together

If the level of comfort is low, handwriting can seem like this for some children:

'Handwriting is like a broken arm: it hurts.' (9 yrs)

To support the production of fluent, comfortable handwriting, use the seating, posture and pen hold checklist below:

- ☐ Is the student sitting comfortably with both feet on the floor?
- ☐ Is the student's seating position suitable for their left- or right-handed writing? (in relation to the table and to the neighbouring student)
- ☐ Is the paper in the correct position and at the correct angle?
- ☐ Is the pen/pencil held in a tripod grip or an effective alternative grip?
- ☐ Is the pen/pencil held with the correct amount of pressure?
- ☐ Are the student's fingers, hand and arm free from discomfort?
- ☐ Is the student's non-writing hand supporting the paper?

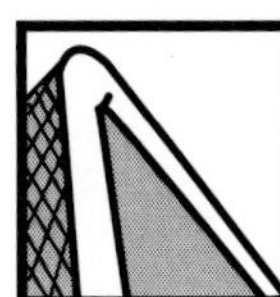

Fixing the Goalposts

Using the checklist

Ideal handwriting is defined by legibility, fluency and appropriate speed. Even so, what seems like good handwriting to you might not necessarily be the same for others. Ask young writers 'What does good handwriting look like?' and they say:

So it's helpful to fix some goalposts. This chapter outlines the criteria for good handwriting in the form of a **checklist**:

1. Use it as a guideline for teaching or assessing handwriting.
2. Adapt the questions for student self-assessment by asking students to rephrase them in the first person. They can then use the checklist alongside instruction and teacher input.

Checklist: Formation

Print formation

Letters and numerals need to be well formed. Each letter has a **set start and end point** that may differ from script to script. The examples show letters in a rounded non-cursive style. Except for d and e, all lower case letters start at the top.

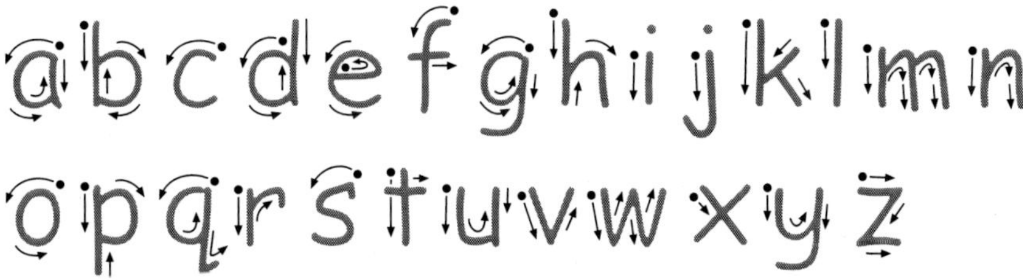

Checklist: Formation

Print formation

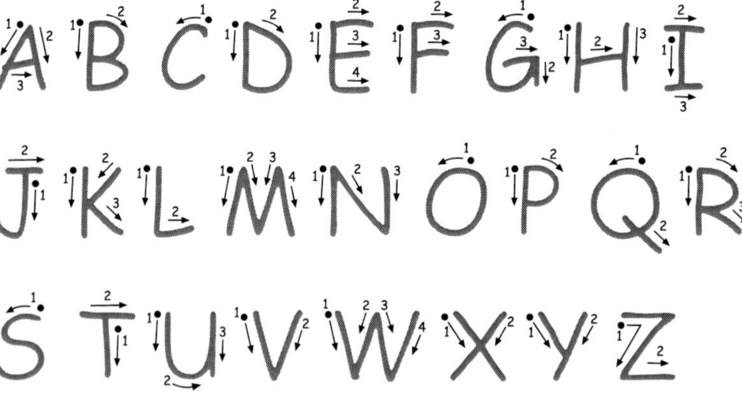

Checklist: Formation

Left-handed print formation

There are differences in how left- and right-handers move the pen across the page. When making left to right strokes in letter formation:

- Right-handers naturally **pull** their pens from **left to right**
- Left-handers effectively **push** their pens from **left to right**

This can cause some problems for left-handers, with the pen digging into the paper and interrupting the fluency of the writing. Left-handers have found that modifying the formation of certain letters, moving instead from right to left, can assist in overcoming this difficulty.

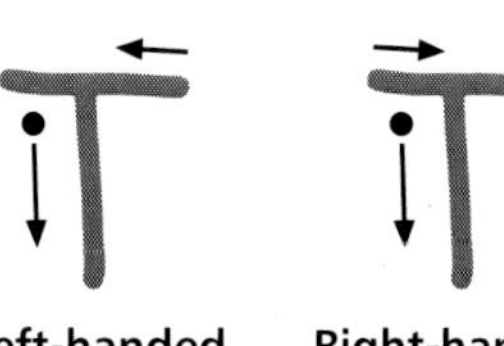

Checklist: Formation

Left-handed print formation

Other letters affected are: Capitals: A E F H I J M N V W and lower case: f t:

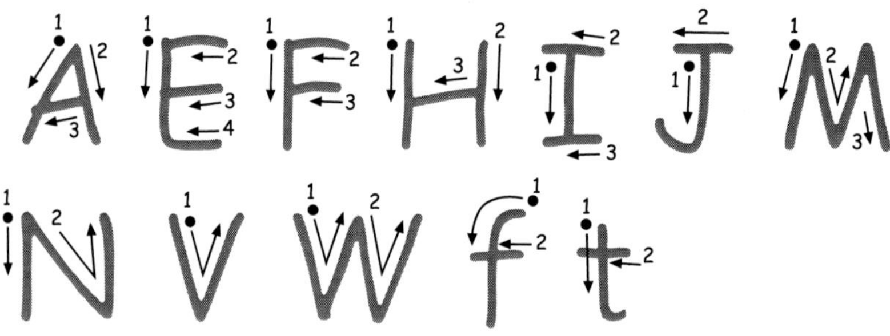

The letters above have been used with kind permission of Keith and Lauren Milsom and are available in the e-book 'Left-handed Letter Formation for Kids' downloadable from www.lefthandedchildren.org. It offers basic guidance on writing left-handed and provides detailed letter formation practice pages. Whilst some left-handers will have their own variations, this is a very useful resource for left-handed students (and right-handed teachers!).

Checklist: Formation

Cursive form

Different cursive styles have been popular at different times and in different countries. There is no one 'right way' of doing it. Some teachers will use a style in line with a particular scheme. Between (and even within) cursive models there can be alternatives or variations of:

- Letter formations (eg: f, s, r) *f f f s s s r r*
- Open or closed letters (eg: b, p) *b b p p*
- Loops or no loops (k) *k k k*
- Joins to and from different letters (egg) *egg egg*

'Correct' formation depends on the script, scheme or copy books you are using. Essentially, it is important to remember that cursive writing is about joining one letter to another for fluency and speed. Guidelines on joining are covered on page 53.

Checklist: Formation

Cursive form

Here is an example of round hand cursive writing.

This is an example of a round hand cursive style.

Formation

- ☐ Are all lower case letters formed correctly according to the scheme you are using?
- ☐ Are all numerals formed correctly?
- ☐ Are all upper case letters formed correctly according to the scheme you are using?

Checklist: Size

There are three groups of letters according to height. **The letters in each group should be similar sizes**:

1. Letters with no ascenders or descenders: a c e i m n o r s u v w x z
2. Letters with ascenders: b d f h k l (and the letter t, which is usually the 'odd one out' by having a slightly shorter ascender)
3. Letters with descenders: g j p q y (and sometimes z and f, depending on the script, eg: ʒ and ƒ or f)

The body of the letters (regardless of ascenders and descenders) should be of similar size. This is sometimes referred to as the 'x' height.

Size

- ☐ Are the letters the correct height?
- ☐ Are the ascenders and descenders appropriate lengths?
- ☐ Is the body of each letter of similar size?

Checklist: Slope

Slope or 'slant' refers to the direction in which letters are leaning. This is down to personal choice: writing can lean forwards or backwards or be upright. What is important for overall neatness and legibility is **uniformity** of direction. **Parallel strokes** for ascenders and descenders help to create uniformity. In the example below the slope is consistent, so the writing looks neat:

There were lots of horses, frogs, dogs and flowers but I thought you'd like this one.

It is not necessary to impose a particular slant on writers unless the one they are using is causing them problems.

Slope

- ☐ Is the slope of the body of the letters uniform?
- ☐ Are all ascenders and descenders parallel?
- ☐ Is the slope of the writing leaning in the same direction?

Checklist: Spacing

'Spacing' refers to spaces between both letters and words. Spacing should be **relative to the overall size of the writing and consistent**. Consistent spacing makes writing easier to read. As handwriting matures the spaces usually become smaller.

Teachers sometimes encourage young children learning to write to insert a finger between words to mark the space. As writers mature it is helpful to describe the spaces as being the same size as a single letter 'o' or as two letter 'o's together.

Spacing

- ☐ Is the spacing between **letters** regular?
- ☐ Is the spacing between **words** regular?
- ☐ Is the spacing neither too **large** nor too **small** for the writing?

Checklist: Sitting on the line

Letters need to sit on the **base line correctly**.

- a b c d e h i k l m n o r s t u v w x z – all sit on the base line
- g j p q y (and f and z sometimes, depending on script, eg: ʒ and ſ or ƒ) sit on the base line with their descenders hanging down like legs/tails swinging below the line
- Capital letters – all sit on the base line

Sitting on the line

- ☐ Are the letters sitting on the base line correctly?
- ☐ Are descenders hanging down correctly?
- ☐ Are capitals sitting on the base line correctly?

Checklist: Smooth connections

When teaching cursive script, there are **two main types of joining stroke: diagonal and horizontal**.

1. **Diagonal joins:** letters that finish at the bottom join diagonally

   a. Diagonal joins to letters without ascenders

   ea ar mo ca

   b. Diagonal joins to letters with ascenders

   th al ab

2. **Horizontal joins:** letters that finish at the top join horizontally

   c. Horizontal joins to letters without ascenders o r v w (and sometimes f)

   wo wi oi ou

   d. Horizontal joins to letters with ascenders

   ol wh ot

Checklist: Smooth connections

Be aware that:

- Many scripts do not join letters that finish to the left: s b j g y
- The formation of letter 'e' depends on where the preceding letter finishes. For example, if the preceding letter is 'v', then 'e' will have a more traditional formation. If the preceding letter is 'a', then 'e' will look more like a loop

ae ve

Smooth connections

- [ ] Are diagonal joins used correctly?
- [ ] Are horizontal joins used correctly?

Checklist: Fluency

By fluency I mean **smooth movements performed with ease and at an appropriate rate** – effortless, unhindered and flowing.

Beginner writers usually have less fluency than mature writers. Fluency is one of the goals we are aiming for, and assessment of fluency will depend very much on the developmental level of the writer.

Fluency

- ☐ Is the writing at an appropriate rate for the developmental level of the writer?
- ☐ Is the writing fluent? Is there a bounce or rhythm to it?
- ☐ Is the writing speed so fast that it jumbles up and becomes illegible?
- ☐ Is the writing speed so slow that it's laboured and the writer is taking much longer than peers to complete the task?
- ☐ Is writing comfortable?
- ☐ Is the writing disjointed or stilted?

Checklist summary – visual association

I ask students to list the eight key words or phrases from the checklist, then think of a symbol or picture for each: Comfort, Formation, Size, Slope, Spacing, Sitting on the line, Smooth Connections, Fluency.

They then draw their symbolic representations and label them with the key words or phrases. This way they have a checklist mnemonic to help with self-assessment and monitoring.

When students have both key words and key pictures they experience a form of multi-sensory learning. Some learners recall the pictures more effectively than the words and some make links between the pictures to construct a story that helps them recall the key information. (When memorising the pictures, the focus for all learners should be on understanding what the pictures mean or represent.)

Checklist summary – visual association

Symbol	Association/link	Representing
Elephant	Size	Size of letters appropriate
Skier on a slope	Slope	Slope of ascenders and descenders parallel Slope consistent
Washing line	Sitting on the line	Letters sitting on the line
Liquidiser	Fruit smoothie	Smooth connections between letters
Parked cars	Space between cars	Space between letters and words appropriate
Red Arrows flying in formation	Formation	Letters formed correctly
Wavy line encircling everything	Smooth fluent lines	Fluency and speed
Armchair	Comfort	Comfortable writing

Checklist summary – visual association

Size

Slope

Formation

Sitting on the line

Comfort

Smooth(ies)

Spacing

Fluency

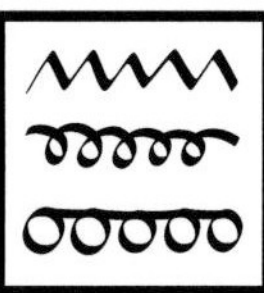

Teaching Beginner Writers

Starting out

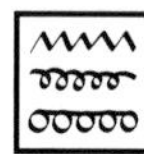

Establishing a positive partnership between teachers and parents is particularly important when teaching handwriting. Parents and carers need to know the school policy, scheme and script. This enables correct teaching and means consistent patterns of movement and motor memory can be embedded at home and school **from the start**.

Offering parents a handout or booklet with the correct formation of letters, or a training evening on 'handwriting for beginner writers' can be beneficial.

Beginner writers are immersed in a process of learning language by hand alongside language by ear, eyes and mouth.

This chapter on teaching beginner writers covers:

- Stages of writing
- The language of handwriting
- Activities for developing handwriting skills
- Readiness for writing
- Handwriting lines

Stages of writing

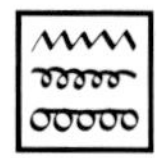

When children begin to write, they progress through stages. Rates of progress will vary according to developmental stage.

1. In the **pre-literate phase** children produce **drawings** as a means of communicating stories and information. They also produce **scribbling** and then scribbling with a bounce and flow, mimicking mature writing.
2. In the **early emergent phase** children produce **letter-like forms**, marks which look like letters but are not actually letters.
3. In the **emergent phase** children produce **random letters in strings**. Some of these letters will be known from their own names.
4. In the **transitional phase** children produce **writing with unconventional, 'invented' or simple phonetic spelling forms**, often predominantly consonants.
5. In the **fluency phase** children move towards developing a more **mature level** of writing, developing **fluency** and **formal literacy skills**.

The activities for developing handwriting skills in this chapter are relevant to a variety of stages, as indicated. You'll also find some of them useful further down the line for correcting poor letter formation.

Pre-writing activities

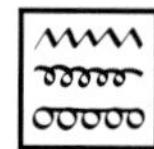

Many of the activities which take place in the early years, eg finger painting, dot-to-dot, modelling, bead threading, cutting, mazes, tracing, drawing, etc, **directly** and **indirectly** nurture vital pre-writing skills. They:

Develop fine motor skills (small movements)

Develop hand eye co-ordination

Improve pencil control

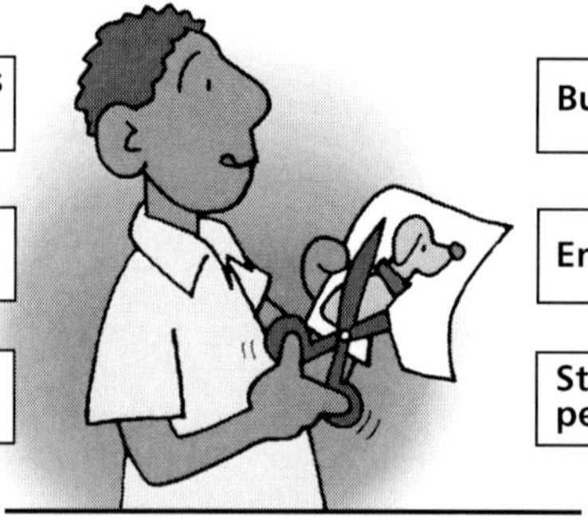

Build up hand strength

Enhance self-confidence

Strengthen perceptual skills

www.absorbentminds.co.uk sells a variety of products to help develop these skills.

Readiness for writing

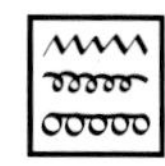

Some children are ready to learn language by hand sooner than others. If a child has general or specific developmental delays in language, literacy or physical development they may need more practice with pre-writing skills before they are ready to write. Ask yourself: *'Does the child have the physical co-ordination to hold and control a pencil or pen?'*

You can gauge this by demonstrating how to draw the shapes below and then asking the child to draw them free hand. A child who does so with control is usually ready for language by hand. (The triangle is the most advanced shape and is likely to be achieved by children over the age of 5 years and 3 months.)

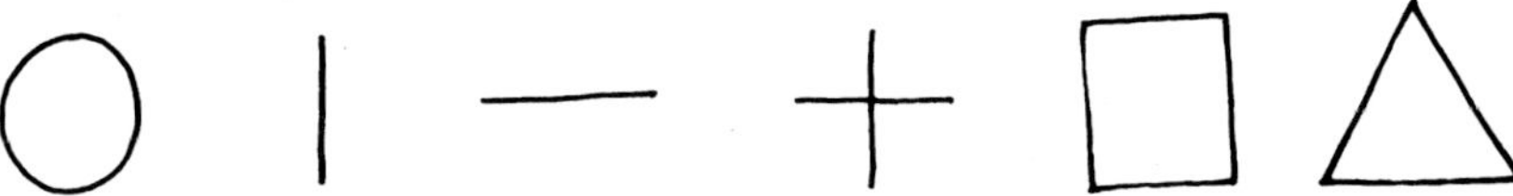

It is worth monitoring a child who has persistent difficulties with visuo-motor skills. They may need more evaluation, intervention or referral to a specialist, to prevent the further development of handwriting difficulties or other educational problems.

Pencil control

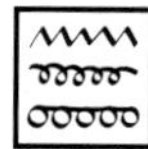

During the stages of **pre-writing and early emergent writing** children develop writing confidence and pencil control. To assist with this, you can draw paths or mazes for them to practise with. Even better, they can design them for each other.

In this example, writers follow the path with their pencil to help the dog find the bone without touching the sides of the path. Narrower paths can be drawn as pencil control improves.

The tracing of lines, shapes and patterns supports the development of pencil control. There are free downloadable handwriting worksheets for children to trace, available at: www.senteacher.org and www.donnayoung.org

Informal handwriting patterns

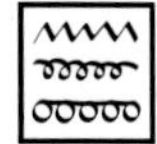

Drawing/producing rhythmic patterns on paper contributes towards mastering pen control and establishing fluency and can be useful at **all stages of handwriting development**.

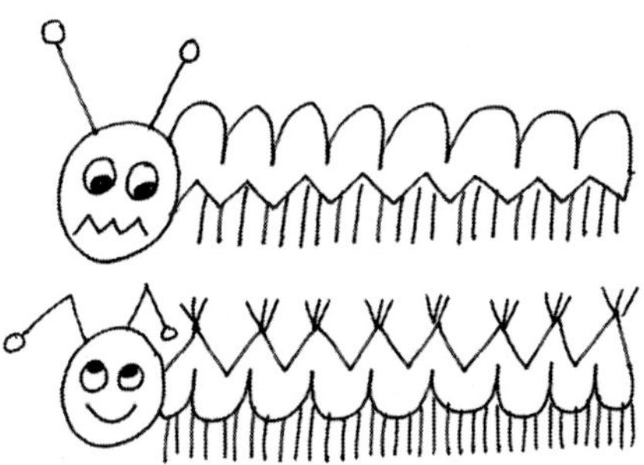

Handwriting Caterpillars
Teach your pupils to use patterns to make up pictures of handwriting caterpillars. As your pupils become more accomplished, you can set specific tasks, such as ensuring that the zigzags are all even or the legs are parallel.

Formal handwriting patterns

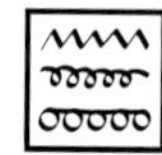

As students move through the **emergent** stage towards the **transitional** and **fluency** stages, handwriting patterns can be introduced to develop fluency. It is important to use **simple** patterns first and then to select patterns appropriate to developmental stages.

Use lined paper for creating series of short patterns (not the whole width of a page) that mimic the fluency of handwriting and the way we lift our pens off the page after each word. Encourage pupils to make their patterns the length of average words.

See the movement – make the movement

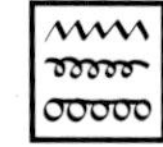

When first forming letters (emergent phase) it is important that pupils see and make the movement of the letter formation and not just the end letter 'shape'. Some handwriting software programs now let you demonstrate the movement of letter formation on an interactive whiteboard which means you can simultaneously observe the movements the children make. (See Penpals for Handwriting p 119).

Alternatively, you can use an overhead projector and transparencies. Try demonstrating the (left- and right-handed) movement and formation of a letter to your pupils. After the first demonstration do it again. This time, during the process ask your pupils to use gross motor movements (big movements) to 'air write' the letter. In this way, the children match the letter formation on the OHP screen. Repeating the process with their eyes closed uses **visualisation** and movement to help **internalise** the letter. Saying the sound as well makes it a more multi-sensory learning method.

Teaching assistants and parent helpers can be invaluable in helping to monitor whether children are forming the movements correctly.

OHP method developed by Vanessa Charter and used with kind permission.

Tracing

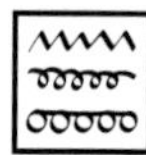

Tracing plays a vital role in the recognition, learning and formation of letters. It is most useful at the **early emergent and emergent phases** when it assists in embedding the kinaesthetic movements in the motor memory and thereby helps to create the internal model.

Effective tracing methods involve gross and fine movements, eg: air writing, finger tracing on sandpaper or wooden letter shapes, and, later, pencil tracing. There are different kinds of pencil tracing, eg dots which form letters; greyed-out or pale coloured lines; tracing paper over solid letters; tracing over letters on individual whiteboards, etc.

Ensure that when a beginner writer says the name and sound of the letter and traces its movement, they are forming the letter correctly. As the writer progresses they can try tracing with their eyes shut. This eliminates external visual feedback and focuses on embedding the internal kinaesthetic pattern.

Pre-designed handwriting packages often have start points marked, or you can make your own worksheets showing start and end points: green for go and red for stop.

Gross motor activities

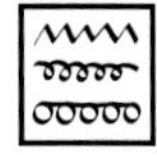

Gross motor movements help to embed the movements in letter formation and promote bounce and fluency. They can be used in the early emergent, emergent and transitional stages, and also to reinforce or correct letter formation with older students in the fluency phase.

Some suggestions for letter formation with gross motor movements:

1. Use hand and arm to create **'air writing'** or **'sky writing'**.
2. Draw and write in sand, salt, shaving foam.
3. Use **water pistols** to write letters on a fence or wall.
4. Dip **paint brushes** (the sort used for decorating) in a bucket of water and write letters on a wall or fence.
5. Use **newspaper** turned on the side so that the columns of text become rows. Thick felt pens can be used to write letters or patterns within the guidelines of the newspaper rows.
6. Use markers on individual **whiteboards**.
7. Fill a **squeezy washing up liquid bottle** with water and hold upside down. Use the whole arm to create the letter movement or handwriting pattern on the playground or patio.

Order in which to teach letters

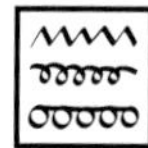

At the **emergent stage** letters can be formally introduced. The order in which you teach them depends on a number of factors. Some schools introduce the written forms of letters incorporated into a phonics programme or according to frequency. Most handwriting schemes, though, sequence teaching according to how letters are formed. This varies slightly depending on which script and scheme you are using. Generally speaking, there are four main movement groups:

b i j l t u (r w)

1. Letters which go down and off in another direction.

c a d e g o q f s 0 6 8 9

2. Letters and numerals which are anticlockwise and rounded.

b h k m n p r 2 3 5

3. Letters and numerals which go down, retrace upwards and follow a clockwise direction.

(k) v w x y z 1 4 7

4. Letters and numerals which are zigzags or straight lines.

The four letters below, however, have different forms depending on the script, which is why they appear in more than one group.

b b k k y y v v

Handwriting patter

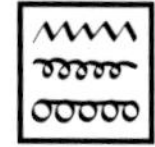

When teaching letter formation it is essential to use consistent and precise language throughout the school. Take care, for example, that children know what you mean by the terms 'up' and 'down'. They can be confusing for some children if you are writing on a **vertical** board and they are writing at a **horizontal** desk.

'Handwriting patter' refers to the little sayings or phrases used by teachers to help pupils remember the motor movements for forming each letter. Patter is an important part of a multi-sensory approach to embedding letter formation in the motor memory. For example, letter 'n':

'Start at the top, go down the stick, up and over the hill with a flick.'

Making associations

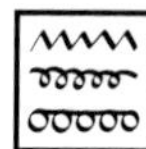

Using multi-sensory methods to teach language is most effective. In some literacy programmes, phonics teaching and handwriting patter are linked with actions, rhymes and characters:

- **t** – Timothy tiger: Trace Timothy Tiger's shape. Extend your arms in a 't' shape to suggest a tiger showing off his muscles. Say the letter sound,*'t'*.
  www.zoo-phonics.com
- **qu** – Make a duck's beak with your hands and say *'qu, qu, qu'*.
  www.jollylearning.co.uk
- **h** – Harry Hat Man: Hurry from the Hat Man's head down to his heel on the ground. Go up and bend his knee, so he'll hop while he makes his sound. Hop like Harry and whisper *'hhh'*.
  www.letterland.com
- **d** – Dinosaur: Run your finger round, up and down the dinosaur saying 'd-d-d-d-d'. Say 'dinosaur' as you touch the foot of the dinosaur. Air write d saying: *'Round his back, up to his neck down to his feet'*.
  www.readwriteinc.com

Lined or not lined?

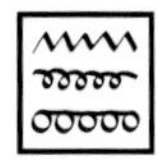

Beginner writers need plenty of practice forming larger letters in air writing, sand trays (with wet or dry sand), salt trays, chalk boards, finger paints, etc.

Writing on lines is a skill linked to developmental stages and motor control. Early emergent writing will often be on unlined paper and this is part of the natural transition from drawing to writing. As emergent writing develops, children can be offered paper with a single line on it for writing and eventually, fully lined paper. Writing instruction is carried out with reference to a baseline.

Eventually all learners will write on lines. They are best introduced when the child's competence, perception and control suggest readiness for formal writing. This will depend on each individual's development rather than simply the stage they have reached in the scheme.

Guidelines

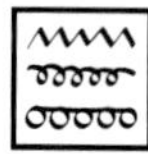

Special guidelines can be placed underneath plain unlined paper to help learners to get the size, height and consistency of letters correct. Many people use three guidelines: a base line, a dashed line to indicate the 'x'-height of letters, and a top line to indicate the top of the tallest letters.

top line
'x' height line
base line

Take care when choosing or making your own guidelines, as very heavy black lines on white paper can trigger migraines in some children and may cause visual disturbance for learners with scotopic sensitivity syndrome*, visual stress and dyslexia. In these cases, coloured or shaded lines may work better. (See resources page 118.)

* Scotopic sensitivity syndrome and visual stress are also known as Meares-Irlen Syndrome. It indicates visual perception difficulties. It is often but not always associated with dyslexia.

Improving Handwriting

Varied attainment

Students come into middle and secondary education with varied levels of handwriting competence. Some are capable writers producing fluent and legible writing; others may:

- Write slowly and be unable to keep up with peers
- Be unable to write at a speed appropriate to the task
- Be unable to join handwriting
- Write untidily
- Write illegibly
- Lack fluency

Students who have difficulty with handwriting say:

'It hurts'

'Keeping control of the pencil is difficult'

'I have to write slowly to get it perfectly neat'

'Keeping focus is difficult'

'It's annoying having to copy'

'It's boring'

Varied causes

Difficulties in handwriting may be because of:

- Specific learning difficulties which can affect writing, eg dyslexia, dyspraxia
- Conditions which affect written literacy acquisition, such as vision loss
- Absence from school during critical handwriting instruction
- House moves which result in changes in schooling and differences in teaching methods/handwriting instruction
- Handwriting teaching in early years not meeting the child's needs
- Lack of practice which is needed for automaticity

Sometimes it's a combination of these factors. Whatever the cause, handwriting difficulties need to be addressed, preferably before they become serious and hinder learning at secondary level and beyond.

This chapter explains how to improve handwriting with the **Key Notes method** and the next chapter gives solutions to specific handwriting problems.

Key Notes for handwriting

At face value, correcting someone's handwriting seems a mammoth job, but if you break down the process, it's easier and more manageable. Inspired by a colleague, I developed the **Key Notes method** to do just that: focus on small, specific tasks for improving writing.

You can use Key Notes with any age and any size group. You'll need:

- A clear idea of what you're aiming for – the **checklist**. (We've seen how the checklist acts as a guide for teaching handwriting; it also indicates the main areas where problems can occur.)
- Some samples of 'good' and 'not so good' writing
- Pens, pencils, highlighter pens, coloured felt pens
- Lined paper
- Music for introductions and a means of playing it

The Key Notes approach encourages **self-assessment and self-evaluation**.

Key Notes: music

In Key Notes for handwriting each item from the goalposts checklist (pages 43-55) is represented by a song which is played as an icebreaker or discussion starter. It then becomes a Key Note focus. I use music in the process of improving handwriting for several reasons. It is:

- Multi-sensory, which aids learning
- Rhythmic, focusing students on the rhythm, kinaesthetic movement and fluency of writing
- Fun, which motivates students
- Participatory. I have given examples of songs with relevant lyrics, but it is even more effective if students suggest and bring in their own songs

Play the music* at low volume, and be aware of students who find it disturbing. Avoid speaking over music with lyrics as this can be problematic for some learners.

* In the UK you may legally play music for educational purposes as long as it is for people in full time education. To do so your school must hold a performing right licence. In the UK the licence is available from the Performing Right Society: www.prsformusic.com

How it works: self-assessment

Concentrating on one Key Note focus at a time, students follow a three-step self-assessment and evaluation process to make improvements to their handwriting:

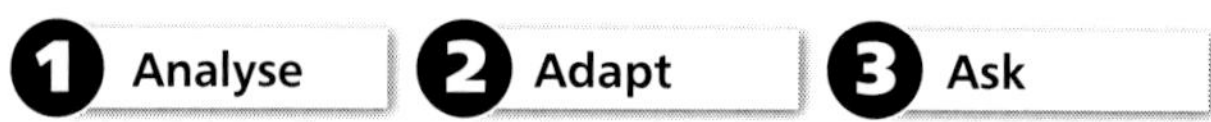

1. **Analyse:** Students analyse handwriting samples, including their own, with a Key Note focus in mind. For example, picking out all the ascenders and descenders with a highlighter pen can draw attention to any inconsistency and explain why the writing looks untidy.

2. **Adapt:** Students then adapt their own handwriting to incorporate what they discovered in their analysis. The idea is to make one small change at a time to see if they can alter their own handwriting for the better.

3. **Ask**: Students evaluate their new attempts. Does it look better? How? Does it feel right? Is it legible? What's my overall response to my improvement? How well does it match up to the checklist? Could I make a further improvement?

How to use Key Notes for handwriting

The following pages contain the 8 Key Notes for improving handwriting. Each Key Note is linked to the checklist in the 'Fixing the Goalposts' chapter. There are four parts to each activity:

- **Key Note:** the teacher introduces the Key Note focus by playing appropriate music
- **Analyse:** Students analyse and illustrate with a highlighter pen how the sample(s) and their own handwriting match up to the checklist criterion
- **Adapt:** Students produce handwriting which focuses on adapting that one aspect
- **Ask:** Students evaluate their 'new' writing, asking themselves, their peers, teacher and/or parents for feedback. Feedback should emphasise the positive changes and encourage further adaptations

Key Note 1: Better Shape Up

Formation

Key Note music	Better Shape Up - Grease
Goalpost checklist link	Correct **formation** of letters. (Pages 43-48.)
Analysis activity for student(s)	Find one letter which is incorrectly formed (in relation to school handwriting policy or scheme). It can be persistently incorrect or occasionally incorrect (perhaps because of the way it connects to another letter). Highlight this letter, either with a coloured pen or by going over the letter in the correct formation. Pay attention to start points, end points and pattern of movement.
Adapt	Practise the correct formation of the letter. Modify only one letter during a session.
Ask	Are all the letters correctly formed? If not, what improvements do I need to make?
Equipment required	Highlighter pen, felt pen, handwriting sample.

Key Note 2: Larger than Life

Size

Key Note music	Larger than Life – Backstreet Boys
Goalpost checklist link	Size: appropriate size of capitals and lower case letters. (Page 49.) You can also use this opportunity to raise awareness when capital letters are used inappropriately in the middle of words.
Analysis activity for student(s)	Highlight under- or over-size letters (or inappropriate use of capitals).
Adapt	Write, paying particular attention to using appropriate letter size (or eliminating misplaced capitals).
Ask	Are the capitals and lower case letters appropriate sizes? Have I used capital letters in appropriate places? If not what can I do to improve?
Equipment required	Felt pens, handwriting sample.

The quick Brown fox JUMPS over the laZY dog

Key Note 3: Straighten Up and Fly Right

Slope

Key Note music	Straighten Up and Fly Right - Nat King Cole
Goalpost checklist link	**Slope:** the general direction of letters slanting left, right or upright, with all ascenders and descenders parallel. (Page 50.)
Analysis activity for student(s)	Using a different pen for each sample, draw straight lines through the ascenders and descenders as illustrated on the next page, extending above and below and following the slant of the handwriting. (You can do the same thing on letters with vertical lines in their structure, eg m,n,u.) Are the lines you have drawn parallel with each other? In which direction do they slant?
Adapt	Do some writing, focusing on making the ascenders and/or descenders and/or main body of letters parallel. Practise with the slant of preference, or practise each style. Follow with review.
Ask	Are my ascenders and descenders parallel? What difference does it make? Which slant (forwards, backwards or upright) suits me best for fluency, legibility and speed?
Equipment required	Handwriting samples demonstrating left, right, upright and mixed slants. Three coloured felt pens.

Key Note 3: Straighten Up and Fly Right

Slope – examples

a sample of upright handwriting

a sample of forward sloping writing.

A sample of backward sloping writing.

A sample of writing which slopes in different directions.

Key Notes 4: Don't Stand so Close to Me

Space between words

Key Note music	Don't Stand so Close to Me - The Police
Goalpost checklist link	Goalpost checklist link Spacing: Appropriate and even **spacing** between **words**. (Page 51.)
Analysis activity for student(s)	Using a felt pen, draw over a lower case letter 'o' from within the handwriting sample. Note its size. Now reproduce it twice in the space between words. How well does it fit? (Be flexible here. For some people the space is more appropriately the space of one 'o'.)
Adapt	Write, paying particular attention to the space between the words.
Ask	Are my words evenly and appropriately spaced? If not what do I need to do to improve this?
Equipment required	Coloured felt pen, handwriting sample.

In the example below, the spaces between words are slightly too big:

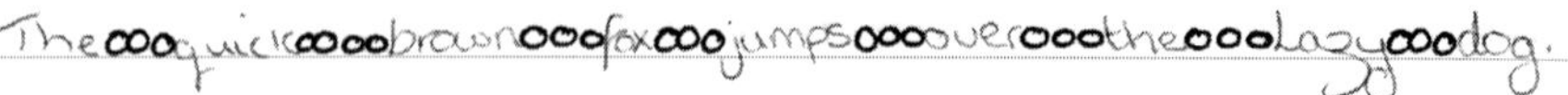

Key Note 5: Stuck in the Middle with You

Space between letters

Key Note music	Stuck in the Middle with You - Stealers Wheel
Goalpost checklist link	Appropriate and even spacing between letters. (Page 51.)
Analysis activity for student(s)	For checking spacing between letters, use a thin felt pen to draw a vertical line between each letter. Note especially if you can draw multiple lines. Does this highlight appropriate spacing? (Be flexible – spacing varies from style to style.) Any unevenness or inconsistency of spacing will make handwriting look untidy.
Adapt	Focus on writing with even spacing between letters.
Ask	Do I have appropriate spacing between my letters? If not, what do I need to do to change this for the better?
Equipment required	Thin felt pen, handwriting samples.

In the example below, the spaces between letters are uneven:

a sample of my handwriting.

Key Note 6: Sitting on the Dock of the Bay

Sitting on the line

Key Note music	Sitting on the Dock of the Bay – Otis Redding
Goalpost checklist link	Letters sitting on the base line correctly. (Page 52.)
Analysis activity for student(s)	Take a ruler and fine-line felt pen. Draw a coloured line along the base line of the text. Using highlighter pens of different colours, highlight: the letters which are not correctly placed on the line, or those which are correctly placed, or the gaps between the line and the letters. (Select one at a time according to age.)
Adapt	Practise writing, paying particular attention to letters sitting correctly on the base line.
Ask	Are all my letters sitting correctly on the base line?
Equipment required	Highlighter pen/felt pen, ruler, handwriting sample.

Key Note 7: Smooth Operator

Connections

Key Note music	Smooth Operator - Sade
Goalpost checklist link	Smooth connections between letters. (Page 53-54.)
Analysis activity for student(s)	Look at each of the four different connectors on the checklist in turn. Find and highlight examples of each in the handwriting sample and in own writing.
Adapt	Practise writing with focus on particular joins.
Ask	Am I using each type of join correctly? If not what are the problematic connections? What can I do to improve it? Do I need to focus on letter formation, entry or exit strokes, or pen hold?
Equipment required	Pen, paper and four highlighters.

Key Notes 8: Don't Worry, Be Happy

Fluency

Key Note music	Don't Worry, Be Happy – Bobby McFerrin
Goalpost checklist link	Fluency. (Page 55.)
Analysis activity for student(s)	To experiment with overall comfort and confidence and notice the impact on fluency, think of someone whose handwriting you admire, or someone you imagine to be good at handwriting, eg Grandma, the Prime Minister, your headteacher.
Adapt	Act as if you are that person: take up the sitting position you imagine they might take; hold the pen as you think they would hold it; behave as you imagine they would and attempt to write as if you are that person.
Ask	Is there any difference between what you have produced and your original handwriting? (Follow up with discussion about capability and confidence and how it affects fluency, legibility and speed.)
Equipment required	Pen and paper.

'Writing as if' originated with Geoff Dowell. Used with kind permission.

Solving Handwriting Problems

Overview

This chapter offers solutions and resources for specific handwriting difficulties:

- Arthritis
- Autistic spectrum disorder (ASD)
- Dysgraphia
- Dyslexia
- Dyspraxia
- EDS and HMS
- Gifted and talented students
- Holding the pen/pencil too low down or too high up
- Left-handed writers
- Letter reversals and confusion (b/d)
- Pressure – too little
- Pressure – too much
- Speed of writing too fast (ADHD/ADD)
- Writers cramp and dystonia

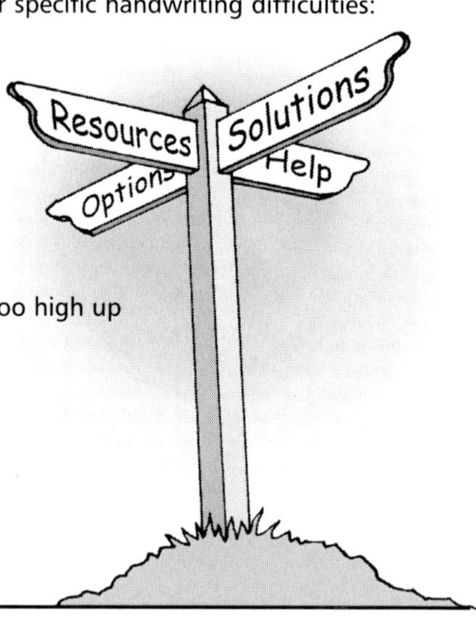

Arthritis

There are various forms of arthritis which occur in childhood. Arthritis is an inflammation of joints causing pain, swelling and stiffness. It may affect a few or many joints. Many people with arthritis keep their symptoms under control with medication; however they can have flare ups. Some students will have painful hand and wrist joints which make handwriting difficult and uncomfortable. They may write **slower** than their peers and need **breaks** to rest the joints.

Occasionally, a child may wear a **wrist splint** or **brace** to support the wrist while writing. Students may also find a **choice of pens** and other writing aids helpful.

There is excellent information for children, teenagers, parents and teachers on the Arthritis Research Campaign (ARC) website: www.arc.org.uk

Autistic Spectrum Disorder (ASD)

Autistic Spectrum Disorder is a neurodevelopmental and behavioural syndrome marked by difficulties in: verbal and non verbal communication; social interaction; the ability to behave flexibly and use imagination. Further details about ASD can be found at www.mind.org.uk or www.autism.org.uk

In addition, many ASD students also have problems with fine or grapho-motor control and motor planning which may affect handwriting. Co-ordination, pen hold, legibility and writing speed may all be affected. Earlier chapters in this book address these issues but if handwriting difficulties persist, word processing should be considered as an alternative.

Sheila Henderson and Dido Green's detailed article, *Handwriting Problems in Children with Asperger Syndrome* is available online: www.nha-handwriting.org.uk

Dysgraphia

You may have a student whom an educational psychologist has described as having **dysgraphia**. Dysgraphia means 'difficulty with handwriting'. There are broadly three different types of dysgraphia: **dyslexic dysgraphia**, **motor dysgraphia**, **spatial dysgraphia**.

The techniques used in this book to remedy handwriting difficulties are appropriate for people with dysgraphia. In addition, you may find that using a style of cursive script where all letters start on the line (eg *'The Hickey Multi-sensory Language Course'* edited by Augur, Briggs & Combley) and muscle training exercises will be of particular benefit.

The International Dyslexia Association (IDA) has a helpful Dysgraphia Fact sheet: # 982-01/00 available online at http://www.interdys.org

Dysgraphia: Why Johnny Can't Write is a useful handbook for teachers and parents by Diane Walton Cavey (PRO-ED, 2000).

Dyslexia

Dyslexia means difficulty with words. Some, but not all, dyslexics have difficulties with handwriting. Some of the underlying difficulties which are likely to affect handwriting include problems with: short term memory, visual perception, decoding, processing, and sequential memory.

- Difficulties decoding (the association of sound and letter form) may result in slower processing speed and cause difficulties in concentration and automatic flow
- Some dyslexics may write occasional words illegibly to hide their uncertainty about particular spellings. (On the whole, though, students do not deliberately write illegibly.)
- Avoid asking dyslexic students to copy from a whiteboard or blackboard. (This will present problems for most dyslexics.)
- Use multi-sensory teaching methods which assists dyslexic students to embed the learning
- 'b'/'d' confusion can be minimised by teaching 'b' and 'd' separately and using some of the techniques on pages 103-4

Dyspraxia

Dyspraxia is related to difficulties in the organisation of movement. This includes motor control issues and may also be associated with language, perception and thought. It is also known as **Developmental Dyspraxia** or **Development Co-ordination Disorder** (DCD). Motor control and perceptual difficulties and motor planning problems mean poor handwriting is common in dyspraxic students.

The suggestions in this book on posture and pen hold will be particularly relevant. People with dyspraxia often have difficulty establishing the correct pressure of pen on paper. For help with this see page 105.

Lois Addy's detailed fact sheet, *Handwriting and Dyspraxia* is available for download from The Dyspraxia Foundation www.dyspraxiafoundation.org.uk

EDS and HMS

Ehlers Danlos Syndrome – Hypermobile type (EDS)/Hypermobility Syndrome (HMS) are conditions where the connective tissues have a collagen deficit. One of the problems this leads to is joint laxity. Joints can dislocate or partly dislocate (subluxation) causing considerable pain. People who have hypermobile joints with no problems, no pain and without HMS are sometimes described as double jointed. Students with EDS or HMS who are affected in the hands, thumbs, wrists and arms may struggle with handwriting. Holding a pen or pencil may cause pain and fatigue, with over extension or partial dislocation of the joints in the fingers and thumbs.

Students who see specialist therapists may be given a programme of hand exercises with therapeutic putty of different strengths. Using pen grips, or pens which place the hand in a more stable position for writing, is beneficial. A comfortable seating position is essential. Consider using wobble cushions, wedge-shape supports, and slant boards for posture. Sometimes students with EDS or HMS write more slowly than average, in which case a laptop should be considered as an alternative to handwriting. For further information, contact the Hypermobility Syndromes Association www.hypermobility.org

Gifted and talented students

'Gifted and talented' students sometimes have difficulties with handwriting. In younger students this might be because of **asynchronous development**. This is where intellect and social and emotional skills do not develop at the same pace as physical co-ordination. Very able students often have a fast rate of processing but if their physical co-ordination lags behind their intellectual development, their handwriting may be slow, poorly formed or difficult to read. The consequences of this for the student are frustration and underachievement.

Some gifted and talented students are described as having **dual exceptionalities** which means that they are gifted/talented as well as having a specific learning difficulty, such as dyslexia, dyspraxia, etc.

Developing fluency and speed will be helpful. The use of visual mapping for making and taking notes bypasses the slow process of handwriting and can be a good way to get thoughts down on paper. Diane Montgomery's article: *Handwriting Difficulties in the Gifted and Talented* is worth a read. It is available on my website www.key4u.co.uk on the page *Why bother with Handwriting*.

Holding the pen/pencil too low down or too high up

Holding the pen or pencil too close to the point can block the writer's view, become uncomfortable, and affect handwriting efficiency. Holding it too far from the point can reduce control.

- A pencil should be held on the coloured rather than the shaved part
- Generally, the writing tool should be held about 2 cm from the point
- To help your students, try wrapping an elastic band around the pen or pencil at the place you want them to hold

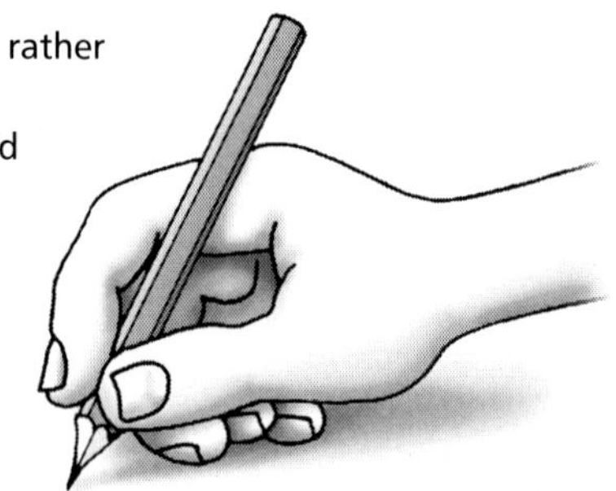

Left-handed writers

Difficulty	Solution
Cramped Space for writing: elbow clash with right-handed student.	Seat students next to other writers according to 'handedness'.
The 'hook' position where the hand is hooked around the pen. The student contorts their hand and arm, with their hand above the line of writing.	Make changes in effective pen hold, paper position and position at desk. (See pages 28, 30-35.) Try varying the standard paper position, depending on pen hold. (See expert advice below.)
Slow, laboured handwriting or cramped writing style, often using all fingers to 'push' the pen, pushing it hard into the paper.	Bring arm underneath writing line; position paper to left of body midline, top tilted; use dynamic 3-finger grip. Practise writing bigger letters rhythmically across the page to promote lighter, faster writing.
Smudging because the writer is pushing their pen across the page.	Change to a more effective pen hold. (See pages 33-35.)
Writing from **right to left** instead of left to right.	Mark the paper at the top left with an arrow to indicate start point and direction of writing.
Letter reversals (pages 103-104) and mirror writing are common in left-handed writers.	As a rule of thumb, if either persists beyond age 6, investigate to eliminate dyslexia, dyspraxia or eye problems.

Left-handed writers

There is a variety of expert opinion about improving left-handed handwriting. A summary of recommendations from the experts is covered in the *Left-handers Handbook* by Diane G Paul. She includes: Audrey McAllen's movement exercises to assist left-handers; advice from Dr Rosemary Sassoon and Dr Jean Alston; different ways of manipulating the pen for left-handers from Prue Wallis Myers.

The Left-Handers Club has produced a fact sheet called *Teaching Handwriting to Left-Handed Pupils*, available from www.anythinglefthanded.co.uk

There is a wealth of useful resources for teaching and improving left-handers' writing. (See pages 114-5.)

Letter reversals and confusion

Letter **reversals** are common in early writing. Some older dyslexic students also experience **confusion** over 'b' and 'd', muddling both the letter sounds and their written forms. Here are some tips for overcoming the problem:

- Work with one letter at a time: teach the letter movement patterns for 'b' and 'd' **separately**
- Focus on the **movements** of the letter formation, not the shape
- Use **multi-sensory methods** to help **embed an internal model** of the letter shape, eg write a large lower case 'b' on the playground. Ask the student to walk the **letter formation movement**. Start at the top of the chalk 'b' (modify movements if using entry strokes), walk backwards to the base line, move forwards and sideways around the body of the letter 'b'

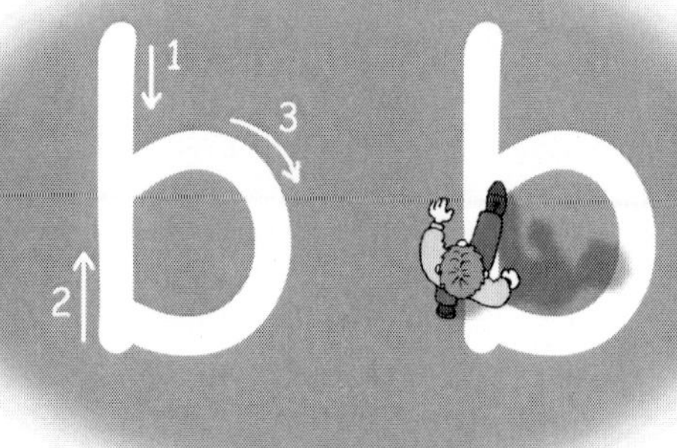

Letter reversals and confusion

- Ask students to devise their own **handwriting patter**. One child's example for a cursive 'b', including the entry stroke, is: *'Climb up the mountain high up in the sky, down to the ground, up round like a fly'*
- Use the 'bed' system to help the student distinguish between 'b' and 'd'. Make a fist with each hand. Turn hands over so that you can see your fingers. Place the knuckles together. Stick your thumbs out. You have a representation of 'b' and 'd' which forms the shape of a bed. The left hand forms the letter 'b' and the right hand forms the letter 'd'. The upright thumbs form the bedposts in the same way as the ascenders in 'b' and 'd'

'The b Box' by Trish Wiggins is a useful resource box for introducing and reinforcing the formation of the letter 'b'. She uses a bumble bee motif to inspire kinaesthetic and multi-sensory activities. Available from www.eprint.co.uk

Pressure on pen or pencil – too little

To assist a student who is applying **too little pressure** on the pen or pencil try the following:

- Use varying numbers of sheets of carbon paper under the writing sheet. See if the student can write with enough pressure to mark through to the carbon paper
- Pens with light-up tops can help students to judge when they are exerting the right amount of pressure
- Ask students to practise shading with a pencil to produce light, medium, and dark areas of grey in a drawing. This teaches familiarity with the different pressure required for writing
- Use a pencil with a softer lead – the writing will appear darker

See also page 39 for suggestions regarding tension and pen hold.

Pressure on pen or pencil – too much

Some students apply **too much pressure** on the pen, pencil or paper. This can slow down the writing process and cause discomfort. Try the following:

- Use three layers of carbon paper between layers of writing paper. Aim for less pressure so the writing goes through the least number of sheets
- Use a mechanical pencil which requires a softer touch to prevent the lead from breaking
- Introduce metaphors to describe using the writing implement, eg *'Let your pen ice skate on the paper'*
- Use a pencil with a harder lead. The writing will be less likely to smudge
- Wrap an unused strip of Blu-Tack®, around the pencil to highlight that too much pressure causes indentations in the blue tack

The Department of Occupational Therapy at The Royal Children's Hospital in Melbourne has a very useful information sheet with tips for reducing pressure on pencil or paper. It's available at: http://www.rch.org.au/emplibrary/ot/InfoSheet_I.pdf See also page 39 for suggestions regarding tension and pen hold.

Speed of writing – too fast

Students who rush through work often produce messy writing. This category includes those with ADHD/ADD, but some students have simply developed the habit of using fast, untidy handwriting for all purposes.

Mature writers tend to develop two forms of writing: a good quality 'best' handwriting and a fast 'note-taking' handwriting which usually looks more untidy.

To help secondary students develop two different hands, explain the need to choose different forms of writing appropriate to different tasks. The need for legibility in both is vital. Try giving the task of writing and comparing:

- A quick shopping list in 'note-taking handwriting'
- A formal letter in a 'good quality handwriting'

To help slow down a student's writing, try giving handwriting patterns as exercises.

Writer's cramp and dystonia

Some people find writing difficult due to pain or cramps and sometimes involuntary movement in the hand or arm. This is called **writer's cramp**. It is usually a result of writing for a long time or of adopting an inefficient posture or pen hold. Tension often makes the symptoms worse. Relaxation and adjusting the position of paper and pen hold will be helpful. (See pages 31-35.)

Dystonia is a **neurological movement disorder**. It causes involuntary muscle contractions which lead the affected parts of the body to develop abnormal movements or postures, with or without tremors. Dystonia can affect just one part of the body or several different areas. There are numerous types of dystonia. One form is commonly referred to as **Dystonic Writer's Cramp**. This affects the muscles of the hand and arm. A specialist will be able to help 'retrain' muscles and 'unwind' the problems with hand posture and pressure. Some people will benefit from medication to help reduce the symptoms of dystonic writer's cramp.

The Dystonia Society has some useful information on their website including an article called: *Coping With Simple Writer's Cramp* by Rosemary Sassoon.
www.dystonia.org.uk

Handwriting Directory

Standardised handwriting assessment tools

Students' handwriting speed may need to be assessed for special provision in examinations. Examination bodies' guidelines for whether provision can be made for extra time or an amanuensis (a writer) are updated annually.

Standardised Handwriting Assessment tools available are:

- The PATOSS (Professional Association of Teachers of Students with Specific Learning Difficulties) website has a handwriting speed assessment developed by Penny Allcock, standardised for ages approximately 11-17 www.patoss-dyslexia.org
- Pearson produce a test called DASH (Detailed Assessment of Speed of Handwriting) authors: Anna Barnett, Sheila E. Henderson, Beverley Scheib and Joerg Schulz. It is designed for ages 9 years to 16 years 11 months and is available from www.Pearsonclinical.co.uk

Other assessment tools for handwriting, hand dysfunction and fine motor dysfunction are available from www.Pearsonclinical.co.uk

The National Handwriting Association (NHA)

The NHA produces some excellent resources. In addition to those already mentioned, the following are also worth looking at:

- ***Handwriting in the Secondary School: Not a Secondary Skill!*** by Beverley Scheib et al
- ***Handwriting – Are You Concerned?*** by Anna Barnett and Beverley Scheib
- ***Tools of the Trade*** by Sheila Henderson et al
- ***Writing left-handed ...write in, not left out*** by Gwen Dornan

The organisation offers courses, articles, publications, resource lists and an annual journal called ***Handwriting Today***. The website contains a wealth of information: www.nha-handwriting.org.uk

Pen or pencil grips

Commercially produced pen or pencil grips are designed to help students improve the position and comfort of the pen hold. Some of the more popular grips are:

Pen/pencil grip name	Company	Website
Grippy	LDA **L**earning **D**evelopment **A**ids	www.ldalearning.com
Cross-guard Ultra Ridged Solo Stubbi Tri-go Triangular Ultra	Taskmaster	www.taskmasteronline.co.uk
Grippit	Different from the grips above, this is a tool to assist people who have *difficulty* in gripping.	http://thegrippit.com/
Ezgrip Pen/Tool Grip	The Dyslexia Shop	www.thedyslexiashop.co.uk
Textreme Squishy Kush 'n Flex	TTS	www.tts-group.co.uk

Pens and pencils

Ergonomic Pens	Available from:
Yoropen™	www.yoropen.com
STABILO 's move easy® (left- and right-handed models)	www.stabilo.co.uk www.anythinglefthanded.co.uk
PenAgain™ (wishbone-shaped)	www.gbapen.co.uk
Ezgrip®; EzGrip ResQ®	www.thedyslexiashop.co.uk
The Lamy Safari	www.thepencompany.com
Manuscript Handwriting Pen	Educational suppliers, high street stationers
Pelikan® Pelikano A left-handed cartridge pen	www.anythingleft-handed.co.uk

Pencils	Available from:
Faber Castell Tri grip pencils	www.anythinglefthanded.co.uk
Yoropen™ pencils	www.yoropen.com
STAEDTLER Noris Club triangular pencils	www.educationsupplies.co.uk
BIC® Matic Mechanical pencil	Online and high street stationers
Faber Castell Grip 2001 pencil	www.stonemarketing.com also available from high street stationers
STABILO 's move easy ergo® (left- and right-handed models)	www.anythinglefthanded.co.uk www.stabilo.co.uk

Left-handed websites

www.anythinglefthanded.co.uk – Left-handed products and information for left-handers. Home of the **Left-Handers Club**. There are two short informative **videos** on left-handed writing and left-handed scissors, both available to view online free of charge.

www.lefthandedchildren.org – Advice for parents, children and teachers. Amongst the wealth of information available on this site are some excellent guides:

- *'Left-handed letter formation for kids'*
- *'Left-handed scissors and cutting for kids'*
- *'Helping your left-handed pre-school child'*
- *'Left write guide'*

Left-handed resources

Books

The Left-hander's Handbook
by Diane G Paul
Published by Robinswood Press, 1998

Writing Left-handed: A Guide for Parents and Teachers of Left-handed Childen
by Jean Alston
Published by Dextral Books, 1996

Helping Left-handed Children to Enjoy Handwriting
by Ruth Fagg
Published by Anything Left-Handed

Writing Left-handed... Write in, Not Left Out
by Gwen Dornan
Published by The National Handwriting Association

Writing scheme

Left-handed Writing Skills:
A specially designed programme of techniques and practice for left-handers, with guidelines for parents and teachers.
By Mark and Heather Stewart

Resources

Left Write Guide Mat
www.anythinglefthanded.co.uk

Left-handed Children: A guide for teachers and parents
(video/DVD)
www.leftshoponline.co.uk

Handwriting resources

Multi-Sensory Learning www.msl-online.net has a good selection of handwriting resources including: *Handwriting Rescue Scheme* (photocopiable masters) and *The MSL Handwriting Kit* (for individual use), a handwriting activity workbook.

Kath Balcombe Educational Resources has a variety of handwriting products including *The Handwriting File* (software and photocopiable practice worksheets). www.kber.co.uk

Computerised fonts

You can create your own handwriting resources by using fonts on the computer:

- Kath Balcombe fonts www.kber.co.uk
- Rosemary Sassoon's fonts www.sassoonfont.co.uk/
- Nelson Handwriting Font www.nelsonthornes.com

Free resources

The Right Write free Handwriting Resource pack for teachers of 7-11 year old students, (left and right-handed) is written by STABILO in conjunction with the National Handwriting Association and Anything Left-Handed. Available from marketing@stabilo.co.uk or available to download from: www.lefthandedchildren.org under 'Handwriting Lesson Plans for Teachers'.

Create **handwriting worksheets** with a free online resource at: www.handwritingworksheets.com. Select from dot trace, dash trace or hollow trace. Scripts available are: Basic print, D'Nealian style or cursive. You type in text and your worksheet is produced with that text. Worksheets show letter formation start points.

Handwriting paper and books

Shaded handwriting guidelines are available as A4 pads of paper or as exercise books from www.msl-online.net

Handwriting guidelines are available free of charge at www.scribblers.co.uk. You can type in different measurements indicating how far apart you want the lines.

Rapid English produce A4 handwriting guideline paper in the form of tear off pads. They are available in four different sizes of guidelines. www.rapidenglish.com

SEN Teacher www.senteacher.org offers you the opportunity to create your own free handwriting worksheets in their 'Literacy Printables Collection'. You have the choice of a variety of text, font styles and sizes and a selection of guideline colours. They are available at: www.senteacher.org/print/literacy/

Printable handwriting guidelines (created and contributed by teachers) are available free of charge at www.primaryresources.co.uk. They have a variety of handwriting resources including handwriting guidelines and handwriting page templates. They can be found at www.primaryresources.co.uk/english/englishA5.htm

Computer-based resources

Rapid English offers an interactive computer-based resource for handwriting which encourages self-assessment and self-improvement. Part of their communication course, it is a pc based product where students can select appropriate sections, focus on six key problem areas, print off guided writing sheets and record their self-assessment. It is designed for ages 7 to adult. www.rapidenglish.com

Penpals for Handwriting is a product available on CD-ROMs for early years and primary settings. The emphasis is on whole class teaching using an interactive whiteboard. The software offers demonstrations to learners so they can see the letter formation on the screen. The program includes reference to left- and right-handers, activities including warm up, music and motor co-ordination. www.cambridge.org/uk You will find a demo video on You Tube at www.youtube.com/watch?v=z8doaJvlD50

Writing slopes

A **writing slope** may help students to maintain a better posture and supports the whole arm, hand and wrist. A slope is especially useful for people with a tremor. The best angle for the slope varies from person to person. Many specialist suppliers, as well as educational suppliers, sell writing slopes, eg:

LDA (Angled writing slope and Clear Writing slope)	www.ldalearning.com
HOPE Education (Angled Writing Aid)	www.hope-education.co.uk
The Dyslexia Shop (Writing Slopes)	www.thedyslexiashop.co.uk
Posturite (Slopes)	www.posturite.co.uk

For handwriting practice **The Wedge Jotter** is a useful magnetic dry-wipe whiteboard which can be raised at the back to produce a sloped effect. www.the-wedge.co.uk.

Or you can create your own slope using a partially filled A4 ring binder.

Write-on, wipe-off boards

Synergy Learning Products Limited produce various **laminated, write-on, wipe-off reversible** cards, some with dots, lines and mazes to develop pencil control, and a cursive handwriting practice card with all letters starting at baseline.
www.synergy-group.co.uk

Learning Space produce **A4 dry erase boards** with guidelines for handwriting.
www.learningspaceeni.co.uk

Multi-Sensory Learning (MSL) has an **Active Learning Placemat** range. Look at the *Early Years Letter Fun* pack which includes letter recognition and sequencing activities.
www.msl-online.net

Taskmaster sells numerous handwriting resources including a large size (635 x 914 mm) **handwriting demonstration sheet, Copy Cat cards** and **guide writing paper**. www.taskmasteronline.co.uk

Kinaesthetic handwriting programmes

Write Dance by Ragnhild Oussoren is a music and movement programme for the development of pre-writing and writing skills in children. The programme uses rhythm and music to develop rhythmic practice using gross and fine motor movement. There are other titles in the series: ***More Write Dance*** and ***Write Dance in the Nursery*** (A pre-writing programme for 3 – 5 year olds).

Speed Up! by Lois Addy is a kinaesthetic programme to develop fluent writing for children aged 8-13. The eight-week programme develops kinaesthetic awareness through multi-sensory activities and exercise.

The Peterson method is a movement-based strategy for the teaching of handwriting. It facilitates automated handwriting movements by developing an internal handwriting model. www.peterson-handwriting.com

Early writing

There are many excellent products available to assist in developing pre-writing and early writing skills. I have highlighted just a few of them:

- The **Pre-writing Motor Skills Boards** from TTS help prepare children for the fundamentals of writing. www.tts-group.co.uk
- GLS Educational Supplies sells the **Rol 'n' Write Alphabet** which demonstrates letter formation in a unique way. The child places a ball bearing on an arrow marking the starting place and it rolls through the correct formation of the letter. www.glsed.co.uk
- **Tactile sandpaper letters and numbers** are available from Hope Education www.hope-education.co.uk and from Absorbent Minds Montessori www.absorbentminds.co.uk
- Nan Barchowsky produces **Beginners' Handwriting**, a set of 28 large (28 x 43 cm) sheets, with a Teacher's Guide. The sheets are put on easels for children to trace and copy large patterns and letters. www.bfhhandwriting.com

Raised lines and wristbands

Raised line paper may help some learners with persistent control difficulties it can be especially useful for children with dyspraxia or sight loss. The slightly raised lines provide tactile as well as visual feedback for learners. (It comes in various forms and is available from www.taskmasteronline.co.uk or the RNIB (Royal National Institute of Blind People) www.rnib.org.uk)

Angle of pen hold

The HandiWriter wristband, (with either dolphin or football motif) facilitates angle and hold of the pen with a good position in the web between thumb and forefinger. (Available from www.taskmasteronline.co.uk)

Books and websites on handwriting

Books

Teaching Handwriting: A Guide for Teachers and Parents
by Jean Alston and Jane Taylor
Published by QEd Publications, 2000

Handwriting Problems in the Secondary School
by Rosemary Sassoon
Published by Paul Chapman Educational Publishing, 2006

Handwriting: The Way to Teach it
by Rosemary Sassoon
Published by Paul Chapman Educational Publishing, 2003

Handwriting: a Teacher's Guide
by Jane Taylor
Published by David Fulton 2001

The Acquisition of a Second Writing System
by Rosemary Sassoon published by Intellect Books in 1995 is an excellent resource for those teaching children who experience cross-cultural difficulties when they come to write English. The main issues concern characters which look the same as those of their first system and the changed rules of the new writing system, eg when a new direction of writing is required.

Websites

Kate Gladstone's 'Handwriting Repair':
www.handwritingrepair.info

Gunnlaugur SE Briem's website on handwriting:
http://briem.net/ Look for the Martians!

Sparklebox teacher resources:
www.sparklebox.co.uk

'Handwriting is like a play: you can never get it perfect.' (9 yrs)

'Handwriting is like your leg healing: it starts messy then gets better.' (8 yrs)

The hand that speaks gives pleasure to the child for whom it is a 'discovery' and a means of representing something within himself.

Ajuriaguerra & Auzias.

'Handwriting is like riding a bike: once you can do it you never forget how.' (15 yrs)

'Handwriting is like learning how to rollerblade for the first time.' (7 yrs)

'Handwriting is like learning to walk: after long practice it becomes second nature.' (18 yrs)

About the author

Julie Bennett BA Hons, PGCE, Dip SpLD

Julie is an independent consultant working under the business name of Unlocking Potential. She has 20 years' experience in the field of education and has specialised in the fields of dyslexia, handwriting and learning. Julie runs workshops for learners of all ages and their teachers and trainers. For further information about her training contact Julie at: Julie@key4u.co.uk www.key4u.co.uk

Acknowledgements

Thank you to those who contributed handwriting samples, answered questionnaires or offered expert advice, including: staff and students at Junior King's School (Canterbury), Sharnbrook Upper School (Bedfordshire), Two Gates Community Primary School (Tamworth, Staffordshire); Vanessa Charter; Alison Cossons; Lauren Milsom; Melvyn Ramsden and Rosemary Sassoon.

Order Form

Your details

Name ______________________

Position ______________________

School ______________________

Address ______________________

____

____

Telephone ______________________

Fax ______________________

E-mail ______________________

VAT No. (EC only) ______________________

Your Order Ref ______________________

Please send me:

		No. copies
Handwriting	Pocketbook	
	Pocketbook	
	Pocketbook	
	Pocketbook	
	Pocketbook	

Order by Post

Teachers' Pocketbooks
Laurel House, Station Approach
Alresford, Hants. SO24 9JH UK

Order by Phone, Fax or Internet

Telephone: +44 (0)1962 735573
Facsimile: +44 (0)1962 733637
E-mail: sales@teacherspocketbooks.co.uk
Web: www.teacherspocketbooks.co.uk